I0440002

Alligators Don't Know They're Monsters

Alligators Don't Know They're Monsters

A Memoir About Mental Illness

ELLEN CAMPBELL ROBERGE
ELIZABETH ABBOTT CAMPBELL

Copyright © 2016 Ellen Campbell Roberge & Elizabeth Abbott Campbell
All rights reserved.
ISBN-10: 1482069504
ISBN-13: 9781482069501

Dedication

This book is dedicated to my mother, whom I loved with all my heart and to whom I will be forever grateful for making me the person I am today.

Acknowledgments

Elizabeth A. Campbell (1923–2006) is the author of all poetry except "Carcassonne."

Rachel Roberge, thank you for all of your help.

Introduction

This book was written in hopes of reaching out primarily to the nonpsychiatric medical community and nonpsychiatric hospitals, but also to each of us who has ever ignored, made disparaging remarks about, or done nothing about someone they knew or loved who was consistently and continually acting irrationally over a longer-than-normal amount of time.

Time and time again, we've seen evidence of mentally ill people who have killed while in a psychotic state. It still appears to me that there is not enough attention paid to recognizing, getting help for, and properly diagnosing the type and degree of mental illness that some people have.

This book is also a tribute to my mother for the poetry she composed throughout her life but never published. I believe that some of this poetry has a direct link to her mental illness, given her state of mind as I recall it at various times in her life. If I believe a poem has a direct link to a period of her life, it is contained within the body of the text. The remainder of her poetry can be found in chapter 11.

In some cases, if a person is not violent, mental illness is ignored completely. That was always the situation with my mother. She was residing in a residential facility for the nonviolent mentally ill over the age of fifty-five; still, a nonpsychiatric hospital emergency room (ER) admitting physician knew the history of her mental illness but ignored it. He stigmatized the fact that she was mentally ill because when the staff tried to get her out of bed, she refused, and she refused to talk. He did not consider the fact that she was mentally ill; he thought she was being difficult. She was seriously physically ill, but because the staff did not understand how to deal with the mental illness and could not understand my mother's reaction to their treatment plan (none), she died as a result of this physician's (and the hospital's) wanton disregard for human life. This is a true story.

One

Elizabeth Abbott Campbell was born in Alabama on August 28, 1923, during the Great Depression and should have been one of the great poets of our time. Her favorite poetry book, *The Family Book of Best Loved Poems,* is mine now, and on its blank pages, I found that my mother wrote her own poetry. I pay tribute to my mother by including all her poetry woven into her story as I recall her life, so that finally I can truly honor her great talent and my love for her. Those poems not referred to within the text are found in chapter 11.

The effect that growing up during the Depression had on my mother would not be evident until much later, at least not to me. She was the oldest daughter of a young and struggling Alabama couple who were barely making ends meet; shortly, she'd be joined by two sisters. My mother told me the family had a few farm animals, as evidenced by her poems "Old Christabelle," "Ham Anyone?" "Why People Put Up with Grouchy Old Goats," "The Happy Scarecrow (Homeless Person)," and "Tiny Tim." As if the Depression wasn't bad enough, her mother died after the birth of her third daughter. My mother told my brother and me that her mother had gotten blood poisoning and died from that. When you're five, you don't question such things. They don't matter until they matter. The fact that we had no pictures of her (although I have one now) didn't come to my mind. Much, much later, after my mother had been diagnosed with paranoid schizophrenia, I was told by my father and my mother's sister that my grandmother had died in a mental institution.

Old Christabelle

Old Christabelle, a cow we had,
Was always very sad—
But no one seemed to care a bit—
Now wasn't that too bad?

If Christabelle had ever smiled,
Or lowed one happy note,
Someone might very well have come
On Christabelle to dote.

But no! Throughout her live-long life
Old Christabelle just stood,
Unless forced to move against her will,
And sadly chewed her cud.

Ham Anyone?

Cupid was such a cute and cuddlesome pig
That we learned to love him a lot,
But when came the time to eat him—
How we wished we had not!

Why People Put Up with Grouchy Old Goats

Old Billy was a grouchy goat,
Who loved to butt folks down,
But hitch him to a go-cart
And he'll pull you into town.

The Happy Scarecrow (Homeless Person)

See the scarecrow in the field—
He takes no thought for the morrow,
But lolls there happily in the sun
Without a care or sorrow.

Whilst round about him in the field
The farmer sweats and labors
And frets for fear his corn not
Grow taller than his neighbor's.

Tiny Tim

Tiny Tim was a bantam cock
Who loved to strut and crow—
Do you think he thought if he postured so
His stature mightn't show?

With my grandmother gone my grandfather, Louis Abbott, was in a terrible place. With no jobs except piecework to be had, he found himself a single father during the Depression, with three little girls under the age of ten to raise. He had family, but they had their own families to take care of during those dire times. When he found work, he went looking for some family member to take care of his little girls. My mother loved her papa, as she called him, and hated staying with relatives. She said she never felt wanted. She said she was the oldest and no longer "cute" like her sisters or cousins. She was simply referred to as "child" and not even called by her name. Nevertheless, she managed to grow into a smart, beautiful young woman who devoured books, especially poetry; graduated from high school; wrote her own poetry; and to me was the best mother in the world. The poems entitled "The Gods Reserve Their Services" and "Little Girl Lost" speak to her pain at this time of her life, still fresh many, many years later when she wrote these poems. Immediately after high school, she went to work taking care of other people's children until she met my father. They got married in 1941 when she was seventeen and he was nineteen. My mother's father was totally against the marriage (for reasons I would never know), which caused a rift between him and my mother. He was killed at the age of forty-seven when a car hit him while he was changing a tire on his truck. My mother and her father hadn't spoken in some time, and it left quite the scar on my mother's psyche, even though I wouldn't realize that until later either. I believe the poem entitled "Memorial Day" was about my mother's father, because he had served in World War I.

The Gods Reserve their Services

When as a child I played
Beside the babbling brook
I could see the handiwork of God
Where'er I chose to look,
And when at night I knelt to pray
Beside my childhood bed
I had no doubt a heavenly hand
Reached down to touch my head.

But scarce the fairness of my youth
Had faded from my brow
Till, "God," I cried, "Oh God!" I prayed,
"Where art thou biding now?"

No answer I expected—
No answer did I get—
For the Gods reserve their services
For those who serve them yet.

Little Girl Lost

"Child" they used to say
When I was a little girl—
With thin straight hair
That would not curl,
And skinny little legs,
And skinny little arms
(And none of my cousin's cherubic charms),
"Child" they used to say,
"Run out and play and don't go dogging my footsteps
The live long day!"

Memorial Day

Beloved, beloved,
My heart cries
Across the chasm
Of the years
Till I see your face again, salt, futile tears.

I linger long
In this quiet place,
Remembering joys we knew,
Till the living call
And I must go
Afresh bereaved of you.

My father was quite the charmer. After only completing the eighth grade, he had a good job as a self-taught projectionist at the only movie theater in his extremely small town. But as wars will do, World War II took my father and placed him on a navy destroyer, leaving a pregnant wife who lived over the local drugstore downtown. After my mother and father divorced, I learned that my mother had made my father promise that they would not have children. This went back to the fact that my mother's mother had died in a mental institution. My mother thought mental illness was genetic, and given my later depression, and the research that I had done, so do I. In the meantime, in the first year of their marriage, my father wrote a letter to my mother and a letter to another woman he'd met in port in New York. He accidentally put the letters in the wrong envelopes, and my mother received the wrong letter. I don't know if this was my father's first indiscretion; I doubt it. If there were already other resentments in place at this early stage of their marriage, I don't know.

She stopped writing to him while he was at sea, and he knew something wasn't right. He begged his commanding officer and got a compassionate leave so he could go home to find out what was wrong. My mother was already pregnant with my brother by this time, and whether she ever forgave him or not didn't seem to matter under her circumstances. However, much later, she wrote "Denial" and "Acceptance," which appear to speak volumes about this first betrayal and the last.

Denial

If the sun were not shining,
And cold rain were falling,
And gray doves were calling—

If ours were an old love
Instead of so new—
That his is you—

No! This is not you
So still to lie!
If this were you
Then I could cry.

Acceptance

My darling,
Today, for an hour or two,
I forgot to mourn and to grieve for you,
I found myself singing
As I did my chores
And I threw open the windows
Wide opened the doors—

I swept down cobwebs
With a busy broom,
Aired all the dark closets—
And even your room.

Yes, my darling,
Today, for an hour or two,
I forgot to mourn and to grieve for you,
And tonight for the first time
Since you went away
I find myself looking forward
To another day!

Even though I heard that I was spoiled from different people throughout the years, my brother got the first ten years of my mother and father to himself. My mother admitted to me that she had no idea what to do with a baby at the age of nineteen, but she did, because my brother was one of the finest men in the world. As he grew, she wrote "To Fred, with Love."

To Fred, with Love

It gives me quite a start to see
My small son grown so tall
That he is now the big guy
And I am now the small.

The eyes that once looked up to mine
Must now look down instead
And I'd have to stand on tiptoe now
To pat him on the head,

But to me, I guess,
He'll always be
That towheaded little tyke
That skinned his shins and bruised his knees
The Christmas he got his bike.

When my dad got back from World War II, he got lucky, and the man who owned the Lex Theater in Elberta, Alabama, asked my dad to run the theater. My father was the projectionist, manager, janitor, and so forth, and my mother sold tickets from an old-fashioned box office. They lived in an apartment above the theater. I came along when my mother was twenty-eight, and I was actually born in Pensacola, Florida, right across the state line from Alabama because my mother's physician worked in a Pensacola hospital. My memories of the first five years of my life are spotty and mostly based on my mother's input. I used to sit in the window of the Lex Theater box office before I could walk while my mother sold tickets. Because everyone who bought a ticket made a fuss over me and talked to me, I learned to talk very early and haven't stopped talking since.

My mother told me of my brother's first dog, Lash, named after Lash LaRue, a popular western motion picture star of the 1940s and 1950s. She told me about her having to walk through the darkened theater to get to the clothesline out back, and how I used to hold on to the back of her dress as she made her way from the back to the front and out the door to the clothesline. I also remember my love of the shuffle game played in Schweitzer's Bar, a local German family restaurant/bar where I came to love the hot pickled sausages that sat in a huge jar on the bar while my father and mother socialized, and my father drank beer and smoked cigarettes. My mother never smoked or drank. That would play into her dislike for medications of any kind, especially later, when she really needed them.

All I knew was that I was loved. My mother wrote "Full Words" and "Little Girl to a New Doll" about me. My brother Fred was ten years older than I was, so I was definitely "the baby." I couldn't pronounce *Fred,* so when I started to talk, I called him Bo (short for brother). I can remember his being there and doting on me, too, when I was a toddler. As I got older and peskier, I can remember him placing the "crown of aggravation" on top of my head with his hands and making faces at me at the dinner table, causing me to whine, "Mama, make him stop making faces at me," on a regular basis. Every once in a while, we'd roughhouse; of course he was ten years older, but I loved it. I'd be laughing so hard it hurt when I'd hear Mama say, "Somebody's gonna be cryin' in a minute," and of course I was.

Full Words

My little girl—how full those words!
As birds in flocks—
As deer in herds.

Little Girl to a New Doll

Sally is a yellow name,
And Ellen is sky blue,
Jean is green,
And Peggy's pink,
Now, which shall I call you?

During this time, my parents bought their first home in the Pine Village development in Foley, Alabama. I believe she wrote "Analogy," "Personalatrees," "Lament for a Piney Wood," "Riddle of the Yo-Yo," "Continuum," "Foreword for a Dictionary," "Alley Cat" (about my cat Thomas), "Pretty Pete" (about my pet parakeet), and "Angry Sea" (about the Gulf not far from Foley in Gulf Shores) during this time. We didn't live there long, however. My father decided he wanted to buy his own theater in Robertsdale, Alabama, not far from Elberta, so they rented out the house. The Robertsdale Theater was a disaster that I mercifully don't remember; I only remember hearing about the foreclosure of the theater later, when we moved back to the house in Pine Village. We lived there for quite some time, and it's there that I remember our family being our happiest.

Analogy

How wondrous to watch
The dawning of a day—
To see the inky black of night
Lapse opalescent gray—
And in the east a glory grow—
And spread from wide to high—
Betokening the coming of
The monarch of the sky.

Then, lo! The radiant sun doth rise
Illuming land and sea—
Alike the coming of the Lord
It always seems to me.

Personalatrees

The proudest trees I know are pines
With lofty crowns
And ramrod spines,
But more beloved are broad oaks
That spread their arms
To welcome folks.

Lament for a Piney Wood

Only the day before yesterday
On these acres there stood
The whispering green loveliness
Of a piney wood.

Today these acres lie barren,
A drear sea of debris,
O'er which a bird circles 'lornly
In search of a tree.

Riddle of the Yo-Yo

Around and around,
And around and around,
And up, and up,
And down,
And over, and over,
And over again,
I'm wound,
Unwound,
Rewound.

Continuum

Forever and forever
Like the waves of the sea
Overlapping, roll the centuries
Into eternity.

And around and around
Move the hands of the clock,
While stone turns to sand
And sand turns to rock—
Thus the circle's beginning
Makes a merge with its end—
Else, the hurricane over,
Where goes the wind?

Foreword for a Dictionary

Betwixt the lids
Of this ponderous tome
Lies a treasure
Past all price—

For, of all man's
Apt contrivances,
Words are, yet,
His best device.

Alley Cat

Thomas was an alley cat
Who on our food grew sleek and fat
And in our hearts clawed out a place
Despite his scarred, flea-bitten face.

Yet, though oft he used our hearth and home
While sleeping off an all-night roam,
Still, Thomas, till his bitter end
Remained acquaintance—never friend.

Pretty Pete

I have a little parakeet,
His name is Pretty Pete,
With feathers green, and yellow beak,
And lots of sass and cheek.

Sometimes he flies my rooms about
Until he's quite worn out—
Then, proving true an old adage,
He flies home to his tiny cage.

Angry Sea

Oh how I thrill
To an angry sea!
To a sea that roars
And rages—

And hurls huge breakers
Toward its shores
Like wild beasts
Let from cages.

It somehow satisfies
My soul
To see this irate giant
Give vent to pent-up passions
And dare to be
Defiant.

My dad loved to move until the day he died—another bone of contention in our family. Our moves were from house to house, usually within a twenty-mile radius, except for a couple of times. Again, I never knew or understood that something was missing from my father's life until much, much later, when he died at the age of seventy-two, and my mother brought out the poem entitled "Carcassonne" for me to read:

Carcassonne

"I'm growing old, I've sixty years;
I've labored all my life in vain.
In all that time of hopes and fears
I've failed my dearest wish to gain.
I see full well that here below
Bliss unalloyed there is for none;
My prayer would else fulfillment know—
Never have I seen Carcassonne!

"You see the city from the hill,
It lies beyond the mountains blue;
And yet to reach it one must still
Five long and weary leagues pursue,
And, to return, as many more.
Had but the vintage plenteous grown—
But, ah! The grape withheld its store.
I shall not look on Carcassonne!

"They tell me every day is there
Not more or less than Sunday gay;
In shining robes and garments fair
The people walk upon their way.
One gazes there on castle walls
As grand as those of Babylon;
A bishop and two generals!
What joy to dwell in Carcassonne!

"The vicar's right; he says that we
Are ever wayward, weak, and blind;
He tells us in his homily
Ambition ruins all mankind.
Yet could I there two days have spent,
While still the autumn sweetly shone,
Ah, me! I might have died content
When I had looked on Carcassonne.

"Thy pardon, Father, I beseech,
In this my prayer if I offend;
One something sees beyond his reach
From childhood to his journey's end.
My wife, our little boy, Aignan,
Have travelled to Narbonne;
My grandchild has seen Perpignan;
And I—have not seen Carcassonne!"

So crooned, one day, close by Limoux,
A peasant, double-bent with age.
"Rise-up my friend," said I; "with you
I'll go upon this pilgrimage."
We left, next morning, his abode,
But (Heaven forgive him!) halfway on
The old man died upon the road—
He never gazed on Carcassonne.

—Gustave Nadaud
(Translated by John R. Thompson)
From *The Family Book of Best Loved Poems*

My parents always nicknamed the houses we lived in since there were so many. During the next move, they were building the house that would be referred to as simply as "the house on the hill," which was halfway down the side of the main road from one small town to the other. While having this house built, we had to rent a house referred to as the "Kaiser house." I hated it. It was old and scary, and it had one of those enormous bathtubs with claw feet that was deep and stained. I was so scared of it that I took my baths in the kitchen sink; it was huge, and I was only nine and small. It must not have been long after we finally moved to the house on the hill that my mother wrote "For Sale: House by the Side of the Road" and "Withdrawal." This was a particularly dark period in her life (and mine), when my father, now an insurance salesman, routinely came home drunk in the wee hours of the morning. I will never forget the screaming coming from the bedroom next to mine. My mother seemed very sad to me most of the time, and sadness was what I understood.

For Sale: House by the Side of the Road

Below my bedroom window
The cars roar to and fro
While I toss and turn on my pillow
Wondering where they go
Until, at last, I fall asleep
While counting cars instead of sheep—

Until at last I fall asleep
To dream of noisy, bleating sheep
With lamps for eyes and wheels for feet
A-rolling up and down the street.

Withdrawal

She sees nobody anymore—
She does not answer
The knock at her door.
She does not answer
Her telephone.
She wakes, and eats, and sleeps,
Alone.

Dark blinds she draws
Against the light—
Till even starglow
Grows too bright,
And in the gloom
The shadows loom
Until they fill
The entire room.

One of my fondest memories of my brother and living in the house on the hill involved his dog. Well, it was officially his dog, but Max, a black German shepherd, was my playmate when we lived in the house on the hill. The night we went to pick him up in Pensacola, Florida, he was six weeks old and just one black ball of fluff. The people we got him from wrapped him in newspaper and went to hand him to my brother in the back seat of the car. When they did, I pitched a fit and insisted that I hold him on the thirty-minute ride back across the state line into Alabama. And I did; spoiled baby wins again. Thank goodness I had Max, and Max had me.

My brother was going to junior college in Pensacola, so he was gone a lot of the time. He had a piece of junk for a car that he had bought for a hundred dollars that sometimes got him there and back. He was so ashamed of it that he parked it far away from his classrooms, so no one would see it. But Max loved that car. We had no garbage pickup, so it was my brother's job to take our trash to the dump once a week in his car, and Max got to ride along and then go exploring at the dump. Sometimes my brother would tease poor Max by getting in the car, shutting the door, and pretending he wasn't going to take him. Max would bark and run in circles around the car until my brother let him in.

We had an old trailer meant for hauling in the backyard, and one of our favorite games was for Max and I to get in it and run from one end to the other, making it bang down from our weight like a seesaw. I needed Max's weight to make it work, and he loved to assist. My mother loved Max too as evidenced by her poem "An Old Lady's Watchdog." There were no other houses for six miles on either side of us, and I was ten by now, so my mother would occasionally import children for me to play with. Max was my steady and faithful playmate, though.

An Old Lady's Watchdog

He stands in canine majesty
His eyes, unwavering, fixed on me
And waits for the tone of his mistress's voice
To tell him how to make his choice.

Then he politely shakes my hand,
And wags his tail, and takes his stand
Beside his mistress,
There to wait,
Till I shall leave and close the gate.

We hadn't lived in the house on the hill very long when my dad got the moving bug again. We rented another house while our new house was being built in Walker Grove (which had been a pecan orchard). We'd always refer to the rental as "Grace Porter's house" because that was who owned it. Poor Max. He'd been used to running wild in the woods at the house on the hill. He wasn't meant to be a city dog. Dogs still ran free back in those days, but that didn't stop Max from aggravating certain neighbors, and I remember poor Max coming home one day with a tail full of buckshot. He had to go the vet to get the buckshot removed. It was a good thing that the house in Walker Grove was almost finished, and we had an acre of land there. We put up a chain link fence around the entire property so Max would have some space again to call his own. But Max had gotten used to being a free dog, and he managed to get out of the yard. The main highway wasn't far from our house. One day, my mother came home to tell me that Max had been hit by a car and killed while he was crossing the road. I remember being terribly upset for a day and my mother being sad.

Our time in the house in Walker Grove was when I can truthfully say I knew something out of the ordinary was wrong with my mother. She cried all the time, it seemed. My father wasn't doing so well financially in the insurance business, and I can remember the fights over money, trumped only by the fights over my father going out after dinner to collect payments on his insurance route, which was apparently just an excuse for drinking and being with other women. I hated the nights my mother would get in bed with me because that meant my dad would be coming home drunk, and a fight would ensue as he tried to get her to come to bed with him. That happened a lot, and my mother became sadder and sadder. She also started imagining she had cancer in her leg where she had bumped it against something; it bruised badly and always hurt her afterward. I can't tell you how many times I cried myself to sleep at night because I believed my mother had cancer. To this day, I have no idea if this was a delusion on her part or an obsession, but later, when I myself obsessed over things to the point of not being able to stop, it did cross my mind that this was mental illness.

Then one day when I was eleven, my brother got married and joined the Army. I think it coincided with my father telling him that he wanted my brother's legs out from under his dining room table. I remember many a fight between my mother and father, but there was no physical abuse that I ever knew of. However, there was plenty of psychological abuse. Again, at the time, I had no idea of our family secrets, so many of the fights were already well rooted and simple continuations from one to the next. I was a daddy's girl, and he was always the good cop (probably because my mother doled out the punishment). So when he needed a pack of cigarettes from J. S. Lanes, a 1950s version of a 7-Eleven, I always got to ride along, and he bought me candy. The problem was that it was always just before dinner. I ate the candy, and when dinnertime came around, I would get yelled at by my mother for not eating my dinner. I think my dad did it on purpose. Passive-aggressive perhaps, the way he got back at my mother for some punishment for some transgression. (And there was always a transgression, even if I didn't know what it was.)

Two

Then things took a turn for the better. When I was twelve, my father decided he wanted to move again, far away. I believe my mother encouraged this move, hoping to get him away from all the drinking and carousing. This time, we moved completely out of Alabama to Venice, Florida. My father knew a guy from his insurance company who lived in Sarasota, only twenty minutes from Venice, and he encouraged my father to transfer, so he did. My mother was happier than I'd ever seen her. It was like she had a new lease on life. The insurance business was worse in Venice than it had been in Foley, but there was a local theater in Venice, and my father spoke to the owner about becoming the projectionist there. He started as projectionist and then made it to manager of the theater. When I was about thirteen, he got me a job at the concession stand.

We first lived in an apartment a short walk from the Gulf and the tennis courts. I got my first tennis racquet and was old enough (and Venice safe enough) that I was allowed to walk to the Gulf and the tennis courts, where I used the practice wall by myself. I never learned how to play tennis, but this was at least something I could do alone. I was in the eighth grade, and once I started school, I quickly became best friends with a girl who was also new to Venice Junior High that year.

We later bought a house in Venice Gardens, and everything seemed pretty idyllic. My mother decided she wanted to go to work, although she'd always been a homemaker, except for a brief period when she had worked part time at the Chemstrand Corporation when we lived in Grace Porter's house. She became a first-time waitress at a local breakfast/lunch place called Smack McDonalds, home of the "broasted chicken." She worked from 6:00 a.m. until 2:00 p.m. It was a hard job, and she quickly started losing weight from being on her feet all day. She was only forty-one at the time, still young, very attractive, and vibrant, although I didn't see her this way (until I turned forty-one!) She had to get up at 3:30 a.m. so she'd have time to wash, roll, and dry her hair, and my father had to take her to work because she'd never learned to drive.

It didn't even seem strange to me back then that she didn't drive. Times were so different. All I knew was that she seemed happier and happier, even though she worked very hard. It wouldn't be until I discovered my mother's poetry that I would find the poems "Bittersweet" and "Atmospherics," which were written, I believe, during the time we lived in Venice. I believe my mother had a male admirer at the restaurant, who inspired these poems.

Bittersweet

We finally met—
It was too late—
High walls between
Without a gate

He not for me,
I not for him,
I not his Jane,
He not my Jim.

Not for we two
The rendezvous
The stolen kiss
The "I love you"

Not ever across
To sit and eat,
Nor walk together
Down the street—

But just to breathe
The world's same air—
Each know the other
Present there,

And live, perchance,
By chance to meet—
Late love is bitter,
Bittersweet.

Atmospherics

In the mornings we meet
In a corridor
That's made of steel and glass,
And I am brisk,
And you are reserved,
And we smile and nod and pass—

But my nights we meet
On a golden street
Where the air is made of bliss
And I am not brisk
And you are not reserved
And we kiss and kiss and kiss.

As if on cue, my father decided he no longer wanted to live in the house in Venice Gardens, and they sold it and we rented in apartment in Venice. He started searching for another theater to manage. I had just finished my junior year in high school and was very happy. For some reason, at the time it never occurred to me that moving to a new school in a new city (Baton Rouge, Louisiana) in my senior year was a bad decision. My mother loved Venice and didn't want to move. As always, she ranted and raved, but eventually she gave in to my dad and we moved again.

The theater in Baton Rouge was one of the first drive-in theaters with two screens. We lived in a mobile home in the middle of the parking lot, between the two screens and next to the concession stand. I was mortified, especially because I later learned that people would try to look into our windows. It started to be quite an issue for me. First, my brother and his wife visited once, and my brother was appalled. Then, as I walked across the drive-in parking lot, up and down over the man-made humps that the cars would pull up on, toward the main road, I'd have a sense of dread. As I caught the school bus each morning, I think I was wondering what everyone thought about where and how I lived. I became depressed. But then, teenagers are always in angst, aren't they? Again, we all came as a package deal. My father was manager, my mother sold tickets, and I worked at the concession stand. I have blocked out most of my time there; I have no real memories of those six months, except for being depressed. This would be the first six months of my senior year.

The owner of the drive-in suddenly decided to start showing X-rated movies. My mother immediately insisted that my father quit the job. He objected, but my mother won this round. This was the first time I can remember my mother wanting to move instead of my father. I was happy to get out of Baton Rouge. My brother and his wife had settled in Pensacola, Florida, after he got out of the Army and had just had their first baby. So it seemed natural that we should move there. It would mark the beginning of one of my darkest periods, when I can now say that my depression worsened. My father found a job at a theater in Pensacola as an assistant manager, and my mother worked in a drugstore. We saw my brother and his family pretty regularly, and the best times were when my mother would babysit for my baby niece from time to time.

I attended the last six months of my senior year at and graduated from Escambia High School. It was a huge school compared to the others I had attended, with a graduating class of more than six hundred. I remember nothing about it except being depressed every morning before going to school. I can only remember making one friend, but I can't recall her name. It was time to move again. I don't know if this was the time my mother wrote "Quest," but reading it, I think it certainly could have been because it seems to refer to my father's wanderlust.

This time, my parents decided to move to an apartment in Orlando, Florida. I have no idea why. My dad was hired as the assistant manager of another drive-in, and yes, I worked at the concession stand. My mother worked at Ronnie's Bakery. I met my first husband at the drive-in when he was visiting the manager of the theater, who was like a father to him. He was on a one-month leave from the Army before he shipped off to Vietnam. I was seventeen, and he was nineteen. We fell in love in one month's time. He was the second boy I had ever dated. I thought I would die when he left for Vietnam, but we promised to write every day; if you can believe it, we both did. He asked me to marry him in a letter, and I received my engagement ring in the mail from Vietnam.

Quest

Man's Life is spent
In desperate quest—
Yon, thither, left and right—
Like a child lost in the darkness
He casts about for light.

The smallest spark is seized upon
And fanned into a flame
For shield against a fear so dread
Few dare to give it name.

Three

Then it was time to move again. I didn't really care anymore, because I was just waiting for my fiancé to return from Vietnam. We would get married, and I would finally get away from all the craziness. This time, my father got a job at a double theater in Gainesville, Florida. My mother insisted that I not be just a high school graduate and that I learn the skills necessary to support myself, something she'd never felt she could do. I attended Santa Fe Junior College in Gainesville in order to obtain the necessary skills to become a secretary. There were no business schools in Gainesville, but I gained all the knowledge I needed to get a job at the University of Florida as a starting secretary at the Institute of Food and Agricultural Services.

I pined for my fiancé. His daily letters kept me going until one day, they just stopped. I soon became depressed again. I would obsess about his having met someone else. Little did I know that obsessed feeling I had would follow me for the rest of my life and was all part of a history of mental illness in my family that I still knew nothing about. Six weeks would pass before my fiancé's mother called to tell me that my fiancé had been shot and was critically injured. He had been transferred to the Philippines to heal before coming back to the States. During this tumultuous time, I failed to be fully aware of the further deterioration of my parents' marriage and, once again, my mother's increasing depression. While living in Gainesville, however, she decided to take a driver's education class and learn to drive at the age of forty-seven. She insisted that it not be my father who taught her how to drive.

I was only concerned with my fiancé's return. When he was well enough to travel such a distance, he was sent to Fort Gordon, Georgia, and its best orthopedic hospital to recover. As soon as he arrived in Fort Gordon, I took a bus to visit him for the first time in almost a year. We were so young and in love that nothing else mattered. We picked up right where we had left off. It didn't matter that he had almost had his arm amputated and was therefore in a huge ward full of Vietnam amputees, where I had to scrub up and put on a gown before visiting him. My fiancé was still seriously ill, and his arm had to be cleaned and dressed once a day. I had no problem with learning how to become his nurse.

We cared only about getting married. As soon as the hospital would release him on convalescent leave, we made plans to elope and get married in Ocala, Florida, halfway between Orlando, where my fiancé's parents lived, and Gainesville, where my parents lived. We got married in September 1971, when I was nineteen and he was twenty-one. Both my mother and my fiancé's mother tried to talk us out of getting married because of my fiancé's condition as well as our ages, but nothing deterred us. I had no idea what was going on in Gainesville with my parents even though we kept in touch by phone and letters. I was oblivious to anything but being a happy newlywed.

My husband was released from the hospital and transferred to Fort Benning, Georgia, to continue his Army service. Now I was doing the moving, but it was entirely different. We settled into our lives, living in on-base housing and talking about starting a family. My husband wanted a baby right away, and I wanted to be happy. I had no reason not to want a baby, so we started trying. My mother was very concerned about my wanting to get pregnant. She thought we were too young to start a family. I became pregnant within a year and had my son in 1973 in the military hospital in Fort Benning. I almost died giving birth to my son because of preeclampsia during labor and did not see him until after I spent three days unconscious in intensive care. My mother flew to Fort Benning to help me with the baby.

Unbeknown to me, she had told my father that she was leaving him as soon as she returned. She told me that my father had become infatuated with a teenage girl who worked at the theater and had been teaching her how to drive in the parking lot of the theater, among other things. I would later discover that my father had actually asked the girl to marry him after he divorced my mother and had presented her with an engagement ring. I have no idea what happened, but obviously, my mother found out. This was finally the last straw for her, or so she said. My father drove to Fort Benning, supposedly to give my mother a ride back to Gainesville. My mother later told me he was attempting to reconcile with her after the young girl had laughed at him when he asked her to marry him, which was why he drove to Georgia.

She apparently changed her mind and decided to stay with him on the condition that they leave Gainesville. So they were off again, back to Orlando. This time, my father became the manager of another theater, and they moved into a mobile home park for residents over the age of fifty-five.

Four

I, on the other hand, became increasingly depressed immediately after having my son, but I didn't know why. I sought help from an Army physician in Fort Benning, who sent me to a psychotherapist for talk therapy. What I would learn much later was that I had postpartum depression, which I believe received its first real recognition with Brooke Shields's admission of having suffered from it. I will never forget the stigma she experienced, which played out in the media with Tom Cruise all over TV standing in judgment and opining on her personal treatment choices. Before this, however, women suffered in silence. I attended many psychotherapy sessions. They helped somewhat. The psychotherapists did the best they could for me. I finally decided that what I needed to do was go to work, and so I did. I passed the civil service exam for typing and stenography and got my first job with the government. It helped because I got my mind off my depression by working, although I would still have depression on and off for the rest of my life.

My husband got military orders to transfer to Oahu, Hawaii. I continued to be depressed. I begged my husband to take me to the Army hospital in Oahu, which he finally did with much trepidation. Before the hospital would admit me, I had to verbalize that I would attempt to kill myself if they did not. I don't think

I would've killed myself, but I certainly wanted to die and did not understand why. Neither did my husband, but he was totally supportive. I was admitted and kept for three days while the doctors evaluated my mental state. After three days I was released, following a few group therapy sessions with an assortment of other people who were depressed for a variety of reasons but none having to do with being postpartum. I was scheduled for appointments with psychotherapists but was not prescribed antidepressant medication. Per the National Institutes for Health, tricyclic antidepressants and monoamine oxidase inhibitors were available in 1974, but no one prescribed them for me. I just kept wondering what was wrong with me and why I felt this way, and so did my husband. Our family would not learn of any of this until many years later.

This was my first experience with the stigma attached to depression and mental illness. I remember how everyone else in the hospital cafeteria looked at the psychiatric patients when we were paraded into the cafeteria together. I told no one of my illness. We had good days and bad days, and we took each day one day at a time. My son grew into a normal four-year-old despite my depression, with the help of my husband and my son's caregiver. I continued to work until it was time for us to leave Oahu. I immediately applied for another civil service position, and because I was the spouse of a military member, I had no problem getting a job back in Orlando, Florida.

The reason for my depression was still unknown, and my mother's battle with paranoid schizophrenia would soon overshadow any depression I had ever had. However, as I finally learned of my mother's early life, I began to put the puzzle of my mental illness and hers together.

Five

My life in Orlando started off as happy as our lives could be with my periodic bouts of depression. Then, when our son was nine, my husband and I divorced. Moreover, I experienced my mother having what I would later learn had been her first psychotic break. I did not have any clue as to what that was or how to deal with it. This wasn't just periodic depression anymore.

My mother loved that we were all living in Orlando. She loved her grandchildren, and she got to see her granddaughter and grandson in Pensacola only from time to time. She volunteered for many an overnight visit with my son and loved him with all her heart. That could only mean one thing: my father would once again become restless and decide it was time for them to move again—away from Orlando, away from me, and particularly difficult for my mother, away from my son. I was recently divorced and totally unprepared for what happened next.

My mother fought with my father to stay in Orlando, which made my father even more headstrong. He had had a massive stroke in his early fifties, when my ex-husband and I were living in Hawaii, and was never the same afterward. Had it not been for my mother pushing him into completing his physical therapy as well as saving money for their future retirement, he might not even have walked again, let alone worked. She went with him to the theater; it was because of her that he managed to keep his job. She had to help him close out every night because counting money, among other things, wasn't as easy for him as it used to be. He walked with a slight limp as well. The corporation he worked for offered him a job as the manager of a brand-new theater not yet even open in Panama City, Florida, and he was beyond excited. Little did he know they were trying to get rid of him before he was vested with the company. Unfortunately, he played right into their hands. This move was different from all those in the past. My mother continued to object, but it became evident that my father was going to win again. Therefore, I thought she'd made her peace with it, as she always had in the past.

My mother was fifty-eight when everything changed. My mother's life changed, my father's life changed, and my life changed, all for the worse. My father decided that the mobile home would be more salable if it had a double roof installed over the original roof. I stopped by one day while the workers were on the roof. My mother asked me to come over to the kitchen table and sit down because she had something very important she needed to tell me. I just assumed it would once again be her trying to convince me to convince my father not to make the move, as she had been doing for weeks. But I was wrong. My mother began to tell me in great detail how the men working on the roof were soaking rags in gasoline and stuffing these rags into many locations on the roof. At first, I couldn't even comprehend what she was telling me. She seemed depressed about the move, but it was nothing I hadn't seen many times before. She went on to explain that when the mobile home sold, the new owners would move in, and the first time they lit the gas stove, the mobile home would explode into flames from the gas-soaked rags placed on the roof by the workers. She told me this would ultimately mean that both she and my father would be arrested for premeditated murder, and it would be all over the news. She told me my brother and I would both lose our jobs as a result of the shame. I didn't realize how serious this was. I just kept trying to reason with her, telling her it wasn't really happening, but she persisted every time I talked to her. My dad pretty much ignored it, although he wouldn't be able to for much longer.

I would also learn much later that my mother's psychotic breaks were her mechanisms for coping with something she desperately did not want to do—in this case, move again. I can't stress enough how helpless you are when a family member first shows signs of mental illness. And you will always feel helpless, for the rest of his or her life, when mental illness strikes again. Each time my mother had a psychotic break, it was like I'd never experienced it before. It was always exactly the same yet completely different. In the next twenty-plus years, my mother would have at least fifteen more psychotic breaks. I believe she died during a psychotic break that resulted in the nonpsychiatric hospital treating her without the same attention they would have paid to her had she not been mentally ill.

I did all I knew to do and made an appointment for her with a psychiatrist in Orlando. However, I had a very difficult time actually getting her to the appointment. It would be during this first foray into mental illness that I would learn that my mother would not tell anyone except family members about the paranoid delusions she was having. So I had to be her mouthpiece. The psychiatrist believed me, even though my mother would not speak, and prescribed medication for her and sent us on our way. He scheduled another appointment, which my mother refused to go to, and even though I filled the prescription she had been given, she never took the medication. The paranoia continued to get worse, and she became more adamant about not moving to Panama City. I tried to reason with my father, telling him that this wasn't a good time to be moving, but my words fell on deaf ears. He sold the mobile home (my mother had signed off), he hired a mover, and they moved to Panama City as planned. Oh, and in case you were wondering, the mobile home did not blow up when the new owners turned on their gas stove.

Opening night for the new movie theater was fast approaching. My father had rented an apartment, and it was stacked with unpacked boxes. My mother sat in a stupor and lived inside her broken mind. My father left my mother every day and night to tend to the business of opening the new theater. I spoke to him and my mother on the phone, and I could tell that she was worse than ever and he was still in denial. After I drove from Orlando to Panama City to visit my mother in the psychiatric ward of the hospital, I learned of the comedy of errors that had occurred. There was a very young, attractive woman who had been hired by the corporation to be my father's assistant manager at the theater. My father was now sixty years old but still fancied himself a ladies' man. The corporation put its plans in motion to fire my father before he was fully vested and could receive a pension. The night of the theater's grand opening ended with a party and my father being literally dumped drunk at his apartment front door. It was only a matter of a week or so before the corporation fired him for his behavior on opening night, after the young assistant manager reported back all the gory details.

In the meantime, my father called to let me know that my mother had swallowed a bottle of aspirin, and he'd taken her to the hospital. For this first trip to the hospital, my mother had the best health insurance available through my father's employer. When someone you know is hospitalized for mental illness for the first time, you learn that the hospital can invoke a statute that allows the doctors three days to evaluate the person and decide if he or she should be retained in the hospital. In Florida, this statute is the Baker Act. My mother remained in the hospital for approximately three weeks before the doctors decided they wanted to transfer her to a hospital in Fort Walton, Florida, that was better suited for her needs. My father's health insurance was still valid. With my father now jobless, my mother was fast approaching the maximum coverage available in their health insurance as well.

My mother had managed to save upward of $20,000 after my father had his stroke. Little did I realize that my father had resented every dollar that my mother saved. My father was an instant-gratification personality, and saving money was not his forte. Well, now that my mother was in the hospital in Fort Walton, I visited her there as well. I knew she was coming out of the fog of her delusions. That's the way it always was: one day she would be psychotic, and the next day she wouldn't be. I still did not have the experience to understand if it was because of the medications they gave her, which were many and varied, or if it was because she just got better. My mother always insisted, of course, that the medication had nothing to do with it and further, always denied that there had been anything wrong with her to begin with. This was one of the first things I learned about mental illness that no one in the medical world will bother to share with you. You must educate yourself about a mental illness diagnosis. Most times, people's lives are so busy that they barely have time for their immediate families' troubles, let alone taking on the research necessary to understand the mental illness of another family member. I was no exception at the age of thirty with a now-demanding job. It has been my experience, at least with my mother, that most mentally ill people do not take their medication unless under strict supervision. At the time (the early 1980s), I had no access to the Internet, and research about anything was next to impossible. Because I didn't live nearby and I worked, I could never catch her physicians to talk to them. I had to rely on my father to keep me informed about what exactly was wrong with my mother and what medications she needed and to ensure that she took them after she was released. This was not to happen.

Much as my father's personality changed with the stroke he'd had years earlier, my mother's personality changed now, too. Once she came out of the psychosis, there was only one word to describe her personality: angry—especially with my father. I didn't know the specifics of their relationship and how it had changed, but I did know that this was the first time in my life I had ever seen my mother take control of all decisions. When she told my father no, she never wavered, regardless of what it was he wanted her to do. She was also extremely argumentative, more so than usual.

While my mother would previously rant and rave about things my father wanted to do, in the end, she had always given in. With my mother safely ensconced in the hospital and my father now without a job, he dipped into their savings and purchased a mobile home without consulting my mother. He put it in a remote mobile home park in the woods of Panama City. After my mother was discharged from the hospital in Fort Walton, I once again drove from Orlando to Panama City to visit my parents. By this time, my mother had learned why my father had been fired, how the mobile home had come to be bought and placed in the middle of nowhere, and the hopelessness of their situation—no income, less savings, a mobile home that had depreciated in value the moment my father bought it, no health insurance, and no future plans. Both of their lives were seemingly intolerable, and I had to get back to Orlando. There are so many things I've blotted out that I can't even remember the time frame in which the next move occurred, but I believe it was less than a year later.

First, they sold the mobile home in the middle of nowhere to someone for considerably less than they had paid for it. They moved all their furniture again to an apartment in Brooksville, Florida, about an hour's drive from Orlando. I think my mother was instrumental in the selection of the location this time and felt that Brooksville was a good choice for retirement. My father had always had a rocking chair, and that was the only chair he ever sat in as far back as I could remember. I soon learned that while my mother was looking for a job as a waitress in Brooksville, my father would rock in his rocking chair and ruminate over how to get his hands on the rest of their savings. During my mother's stay in yet another psychiatric hospital, I would discover the poems she had written years after my father had left her, and she had been living by herself for many years. "After the Stroke," "Withdrawal," "Hard to Believe," and "Beggar Woman" speaks volumes about what she had experienced in Brooksville and what lay ahead of her.

After the Stroke

Twig by twig
I built the nest—
It took a long, long time.
And then to get the egg inside
I hoarded every dime—

(I cooked and cleaned and nursed and wept—
Sometimes for weeks I hardly slept)
So busy I scurried,
I somehow failed to see
That the bird beside me in the tree,
Rocking slowly to and fro
Was a hawk watching me.

Hard to Believe

The sun will still rise,
And the sun still set,
The wind will still blow
And the rain still wet.

And some other person
Will as well fill the place
That I leave vacant
In the human race.

Beggar-Woman

I am a wretched beggar-woman
A-begging at your door
For a love you cannot tender me—
A love you bear no more—

And though I grovel at your feet—
And weep and wail my woe
I know it will me naught avail
And you will bid me go—

Yes, well I know it's over,
The love we once did share,
Now that you love another,
But it's more than I can bear.

I am a wretched beggar-woman,
A-begging at your door,
For a love you cannot tender me—
A love you bear no more.

Contemplation at Twilight Time

Day by day the sunsets
Lovelier to me—
The closer comes the last one
That I shall ever see.

Nightmare

I dream I walk lost
Down a lonely road
At twilight time of day
With dusk behind me
And darkness ahead
And no lamp to light my way
And from out the unknown
Comes the knell of a bell
Rung long, rung sad, rung slow—

Where does the road lead me?
Where does it go?
Oh wake me!
Before I know!

It wasn't long before I received a phone call from my mother that my father continued to tell her that the day he turned sixty-two and was eligible for social security that he "was divorcing her ass" and taking his half of the money that was in savings. I'd never heard these types of threats before and never really believed it would happen. My mother insisted that I come over and talk some sense into my father. Frankly, it seemed to me they hated each other, and perhaps this was the only solution to end everyone's suffering. The year was 1983. My father was sixty-two, my mother was sixty, I was thirty-two, and they had been married forty-one years. It never occurred to me that just because I had made it through a divorce didn't mean that my mother could do the same, especially at her age and having been married her entire adult life. It certainly never occurred to me that she would have a recurrence of paranoid schizophrenia. I thought that was behind us, never to return again. Far from it!

A few days after he received his first social security check, my father told my mother he was leaving, and he drove her to their bank to get his half of their savings. Then he bought an old beat-up truck with a camper top on the back and packed all his belongings into the back. He called me in Orlando, told me he had left my mother, and asked me if he could come and stay with me a few days before he headed back to Foley, Alabama. I was flabbergasted, but he was still my father. I told him he could come for a few days. When he came, I tried to talk some sense into him and begged him to return to my mother. He refused. After a few days, he left for Foley. He had come full circle.

I called my mother regularly during this terrible time. I knew she was distraught, but I had no idea how distraught. At the time, it never dawned on me just how bad the situation was. Here was my sixty-year-old mother in an apartment an hour away, alone, knowing no one, unemployed, and depressed. The first opportunity I had, I drove to Brooksville. It was nearly impossible to talk to her; she was so upset and understandably so. But here I was, thirty-two, divorced, and in a relationship that would prove to be treacherous as well, with a full-time job that took up most of my time except for weekends. I had no idea how to help her. Her main worries, as always, were money and health insurance. With no income and not being eligible for social security for another two years, she told me she had to get a job. I didn't even question it when she said it; I didn't know any better at the time. Can you imagine your sixty-year-old mother, never really having worked before except as a waitress, going out to look for a job? I thanked my lucky stars that she'd learned to drive, and she had a car that was in pretty good condition. When she told me she was working at a Country Kitchen on the night shift, the only reaction I had was relief. Oh, the things you do not know when you're thirty-two.

It was now 1984, and my mother drove herself to and from work as a waitress, working from 3:00 p.m. to 11:00 p.m. She told me she encountered drunks and insulting patrons. One day, she quit—I can't remember why—and went on the lookout for another job. Once again, I had no real reaction, being consumed with my own problems. I'd talk to her on the phone, write letters, and visit her on weekends. She was miserable, and she made me miserable every time I spoke to her. I didn't know how to help her end her misery, and I felt guilty. She got another waitressing job at a Greek restaurant in town and seemed somewhat better. I think another year passed, and everything seemed the same. Then she started having problems with coworkers at the restaurant. The next thing I knew, she had quit this job, too. My brother would also visit her in Brooksville, but we did not discuss her situation.

By this time, it was 1985, and I was making my own big mistakes and misery. My mother came over to visit me a couple of times and felt very uncomfortable around my future husband and his family. When she came over for our wedding in late 1985, I was oblivious to her growing depression. Six more months went by, and it was 1986. She hadn't found another job and was worried about paying the rent on her apartment, which she still had a few months' lease on. I recommended she take her savings and buy a mobile home in Brooksville. I'd visit her, and we'd go looking but to no avail. Then one weekend, she wanted to go to Orlando and look for something there. I didn't realize it at the time, but she had obsessed about her worries until another psychotic break had begun as yet another way to cope with a situation she did not know how to resolve.

When I visited her in Brooksville, it was as if she was frozen in time and could make no decisions whatsoever. She started complaining about her landlord, saying that he was spying on her. I didn't connect the dots until another visit, when she told me that the landlord was spraying poison on her patio. When she stepped on it barefoot, it was eating away the soles of her feet, and she had to get away from there. No matter what rationale I provided (he was pressure cleaning with a bleach mixture to keep her patio clean), she would dismiss it. I knew she would eventually spend all her savings in rent, and something had to be done, but I couldn't get through to her that she still needed to think about buying a mobile home. I was in denial about her insistence that the landlord was trying to get her to move by all different methods of intimidation. I was lost; she was lost. Then one day, I got a call from my father.

Six

My father had been writing letters to my mother, trying to convince her he wanted to get back together, and he would come to Brooksville to pick her up if I'd set up a mover. I was appalled and relieved at the same time. I knew my mother was delusional again, and again, I didn't have a clue what to do. So I called my father back and told him that she was "sick again," and he knew what I meant. He said he didn't care; he'd take care of her. I wanted to believe him with every fiber of my being so this problem would go away. He had told me on the phone previously that he was friends with a woman we had known when I was a child. I was suspicious. I asked my father if he was in a relationship with her, and he vehemently denied it. I suspected he was lying, but I was desperate for help with my increasingly more delusional mother and a husband who didn't care or offer any advice at all, other than for me to stop talking about it. So I arranged for a mover to come and move my mother's belongings to Foley, and my father told me he'd take the bus down if I'd pick him up at the bus station.

This was the worst thing I feel I ever did as a daughter. I became a full participant in the stigma of mental illness by shirking my responsibility as a daughter and ignoring everything I knew about my father. My mother had been to her bank and got a cashier's check for the remainder of her savings. We picked my father up at 3:00 a.m. and returned to their former apartment together. I was in such a state myself that I cannot remember if my father had already divorced my mother or not, but I believe he had. It was as if he'd never left; they immediately started arguing about everything. My mother was now even angrier than she had been when he left her. We waited for the movers to arrive. Earlier in the day, we had gone for breakfast, and when my mother went to the restroom, I had once again asked my father if he was seeing the other woman because my mother was the same angry person and now delusional again. He once again denied any relationship and told me that he would take good care of my mother.

The movers did not arrive until almost 5:00 p.m., and the fighting between my mother and father had resumed as if he'd never left. As soon as the movers arrived, I left as fast as I could and drove home to Orlando. All I selfishly wanted was for the problem to go away. My father drove my mother's car, packed full of her belongings that the mover had not taken, until they reached Foley, Alabama. The next day, my mother called me and told me they had arrived, and I already sensed that something was not right. My father lived in a new, county-subsidized retirement apartment, so that sounded good. What he hadn't told me or my mother was that he had not informed the landlord that my mother would now be living with him. To most people, this would be a nonissue. However, given my mother's delusional state and her honest nature, she could not focus on any other subject, obsessed over this, and insisted that my father tell the landlord. What I would learn a few days later was that my father had put all my mother's belongings in storage and was, in fact, not only in a relationship with the woman we all knew but was also plotting to get the rest of my mother's savings and sell her belongings. My brother and I were at a bad place in our own relationship. Although I did not speak to my brother, my father told me he was aware of the fact that my mother was back in Foley and had visited them in the apartment.

My mother just got sicker and more withdrawn and started exhibiting all the signs of full-blown paranoid schizophrenia—refusing to eat, not sleeping, pacing, and obsessing about everything. I felt small, miserable, and back in the same "what do I do now?" mode I'd been in. The next thing to happen was my mother's insistence that she get out of my father's apartment. She called her sister and her husband, explained the situation, and asked for their help. My aunt was as clueless as I was about mental illness, and this was her first rodeo. My mother stayed with her for approximately three days until I received a frantic phone call from my aunt telling me simply to "come and get my mother and take her back to Orlando" to live with me. Afterward, my mother would pen the poem "Bitter Brew," which I believe is about how her sister treated her during this three-day period. I called my father and was incredulous to hear him say that my mother was crazy, and he was done with her; nevertheless, I was not really that surprised. I would later learn that my father's girlfriend had visited their apartment daily and would always kiss my father hello and good-bye. They were, in fact, involved in a relationship of some sort, part of which was to get my mother's remaining savings and furniture.

Bitter Brew

There's not a draught
So bitter
As a love that comes
Too late—
Unless it is
That sister brew,
A loved turned
Into hate.

I then called my aunt back and told her that I couldn't come up until the weekend and that what my mother really needed was to be taken to the hospital. Could she please do that? My aunt, whom I thought I knew, turned into a complete stranger. However, in hindsight, I know she also had no idea how to deal with a person who never slept or ate and was always pacing, and spewing delusions. I told my aunt that she had to call my brother, who still lived in Pensacola, only thirty minutes away. I then called my brother myself but got no answer.

As I would later learn, my aunt had also called my brother and gotten no answer. She had then called my father. The sickening plan was hatched. My father drove to my aunt's house and parked his truck there. He then drove my mother's car to my brother's house, with my mother in the passenger seat and my aunt and her husband following them in their car. They got my very delusional mother out of the car, took her to my brother's front door, and rang the doorbell, with my uncle yelling, "You SOB!" from his car at the top of his lungs when my brother answered the door. Neighbors started coming out of their houses. My brother had been visiting my father in Foley since he'd moved back, and he had visited my mother and father when she moved back, but he did not know the magnitude of the situation. He knew my mother had been hospitalized previously for mental illness in Panama City, but he knew none of the details and certainly nothing about mental illness. He was yet another helpless victim in this comedy of horrors. He had two small, impressionable children and a wife inside the house, all of whom were frightened beyond belief at the drama that was occurring outside their front door. My father had brought my mother to my brother's house to dump her for my brother to take care of.

The next phone call I received was from my brother, who told me what had transpired, in what I heard as a cold, hard voice but was really a terrified, out-of-his-mind voice. He told me he'd driven my mother in her car to the hospital in Pensacola, told the doctors that she was mentally ill, and left her there. His wife had picked him up, and he'd left her car in the parking lot with all her belongings in it, except what was still in storage. He had left the hospital only my telephone number as next of kin. I was angry and could not understand how my father, my brother, and my mother's sister could have abandoned her when she was so sick. However, I had abandoned her, too, when I had encouraged her to move back in with my irresponsible father, who only wanted the money she had left. And while delusional, she wasn't delusional enough to sign the money over to my father, and therefore, she was of no further use to him. I was overcome with guilt.

Seven

As soon as I hung up the phone from talking to my brother, I called the hospital in Pensacola to find out how my mother was doing. She definitely needed to be in the hospital, and I was informed that she was being given antipsychotic medications to attempt to control her delusions. This time, I was not aware of what the specific delusions were or if they had changed since she left Brooksville. I did not realize the ramifications of what they told me, and they did not spell them out for me. I had no idea what happens when a person goes to a hospital, is too young for Medicare, and no longer has health insurance. The hospital explained that a judge would come to the hospital on a weekly basis, and there would be a Baker Act hearing in order to keep her to evaluate her condition. The Baker Act hearing would determine if my mother was of danger to herself or anyone else, and the attending physician would be in attendance to give his recommendation to the judge. The hospital asked me if I or another family member would be attending this hearing. I said I could not leave my job to attend the hearing, but I asked them to please keep me informed as to her condition and promised I would be up as soon as possible. Then, just when I thought it could not possibly get worse, it did. The next day, I received another call from the hospital telling me that because my mother had no private health insurance, and the judge had ruled that she was a danger to herself, she could not continue to stay there. They were transferring her by van to the Florida State Hospital; a mental health facility originally called the Florida Asylum for the Indigent Insane but more commonly referred to simply as Chattahoochee by long-time Floridians. I became physically ill.

When I was a child, we had passed by Chattahoochee on our way back to Foley to visit relatives when we lived in Venice. The place had always frightened me because at that time my mother had spoken of it being an "insane asylum." I had no concept of what that was but intuitively knew it was not a good thing. I was terrified for my mother. I took emergency leave to drive from Orlando to Chattahoochee. It was the longest seven-hour drive I had ever made.

I had no idea how frightening it would be. Its reputation at that time was…well…horrific, but in reality, it's not so different from most state-run asylums around the country, I guess. I didn't know if any asylums had the same colorful history as Chattahoochee. From a federal arsenal during the Second Seminole War and Civil War, to the Freedman's Bureau, to Florida's first state penitentiary, and finally to an asylum for the mentally ill, the Florida State Hospital has a remarkable past—some periods that produced scenes one could only find in a horror movie. When you move into the 1900s, the story really gets increasingly notorious—political scandals, patient abuse, use of treatments such as electric shock and lobotomies, and the confinement of thousands of men, women, and children who weren't really insane at all. It was also home to all of Florida's criminally insane, including murderers, rapists, and the likes. They were housed in a separate building.

I followed the protocol for visiting a patient and arranged to see my mother. I saw my brother had visited her, too, from the sign-in log. My brother and I were estranged at the time and neither was available to console the other. It would be our undoing for many years to come.

Before they brought my mother out to the visiting area, I looked in (I wasn't allowed inside) and saw rows and rows of beds with people in them. A scene plucked from a psychological thriller. When my mother came out, I couldn't stop crying. She never cried. That is one of the classic symptoms of paranoia, I would learn later: she couldn't cry. I noticed that her forehead was now etched with three very deep lines that would never go away. As soon as I started talking to her, I knew she was still paranoid. Right away, she started telling me that she wasn't sick, and as soon as the doctors realized that, they'd come after me and my brother for fraud. It was always about what would happen to me or my brother. She was never violent. She was just wasting away, literally and figuratively. Every time she got sick, she was only concerned about her perceived effect on us. She was too ill to comprehend the enduring impact it really had. She seemed almost oblivious to the effect it had on her, except the occasional detail she would tell me about how several staff members had given her a very rough shower. She wasn't eating, sleeping, or showering—again, all typical symptoms. My sadness was almost unbearable. I felt completely helpless. I didn't know what to do or say. There was no physician there to speak with me on a Saturday; I was told I'd have to wait until Monday to get any information on her condition. I don't recall what visiting hours were now, but I went back to every visiting hour there was on Saturdays and Sundays. I was staying in a run-down cottage that must've been forty years old. There were no mainstream motels in Chattahoochee; not many people visited there. I don't even think there was a phone in the cottage, and of course, cell phones were still not in common use until later. I spent the remainder of my weekends alternating between crying and watching television with a husband back in Orlando, who wanted nothing to do with any of it.

When Monday came, I felt like I'd been drained of all the blood in my body. I went early to the administration building and asked to talk with anyone who would speak to me about my mother. I was given the name of the case manager who was assigned to my mother's case and was shown into her office after a long wait. I immediately began to cry. I gathered my composure. I had a lot of questions to ask. How could the hospital in Pensacola have sent her to Chattahoochee just because her health insurance had run out? Who was her physician, and when could I speak to him? What was her prognosis? I eventually got her physician's name, but I never met him. He would only speak to me on the phone. I would call him from pay phones. He would eventually tell me what I would come to understand but not yet. When she had been hospitalized before, when my father was still with her, and they still had health insurance, I had stupidly let my father ask all the questions; I just cried and visited my mother. I never really got involved with her physicians or what she was diagnosed with or what medications they were giving her, although I distinctly remember that she had been on Thorazine, which had made her zombie-like.

This Chattahoochee physician said they had her on antipsychotic medication, but it wasn't working so far. He said she'd have to stay there until she improved dramatically. Right away, I knew this was an intolerable situation for all of us. If they released her to my custody, which they said they could not do, what was I going to do? Take her back to Orlando and try to find someone there who would treat her with no health insurance? Leave her there until she was well? I was inconsolable. I begged the case manager and the physician for some solution that would get her closer to me in Orlando. I was like a little dog biting at their ankles; I would not be deterred. I believe they finally saw that I was serious about helping my mother. I got the impression that most of the people there didn't have anyone to help them. I learned for the first time in my life the necessity for anyone who is hospitalized for any reason to have an advocate, someone who will fight for him or her, if necessary. And I am very sad to say that it was necessary for me to be an advocate for my mother many, many times because our health-care system, whether state run or private, is sorely lacking in patient care for mental illness.

My mother's case manager at Florida State Hospital informed me that the state had decentralized state mental hospitals due to lack of funding and that most of the patients had been discharged, whether they were still mentally ill or not, even if they had no family and nowhere to go. These poor, helpless, exiled mentally ill would become many of our first homeless population. Because I was determined to help my mother, the state hospital case manager decided to help me. She researched all the available resources for housing the mentally ill in the state for me and came up with a facility that was only an hour's drive from Orlando. It was for mentally ill patients over the age of fifty-five. My mother was sixty-two. The state case manager coordinated with the facility my mother would be going to, and she was assigned a case manager there. She told the state case manager that the facility would accept my mother, but she had to sign herself in. However, there was a distinct possibility that when my mother arrived, she would refuse to sign herself in. She trusted no one but me. So I told the facility state case manager that my mother would sign if I was there when she arrived from Chattahoochee.

A few days later, my mother was driven down in a van with other mentally ill patients destined for the few existing mental health facilities in Florida. There was also a dedicated stand-alone psychiatric hospital, the only one of its kind that I know of. The facility where my mother would live was affiliated with the hospital and partially funded by the county. It had mercifully come into existence when the Florida State Hospital turned so many mentally ill patients out. I was told that the trip by van would take approximately eight hours. I arrived early at the facility to await my mother's arrival, at which time I would have to convince her to sign herself in. I was sick to my stomach, not knowing if my mother would sign or not. If she did not sign, she would be returned by the van to the state hospital.

I met the new case manager and spent a good deal of the day talking to her about my mother's specific issues of paranoid delusions. There were three levels of care in the facility. The first level housed the least functioning, the second level consisted of those who were more able to function, and the third level was for highly functioning patients who were somewhat independent. The staff for the first two levels of the facility was comprised of a registered nurse and two licensed practical nurses for each eight-hour shift. The third level was housed in a separate, newer building across the parking lot and had been built after the building that housed levels I and II. There were approximately fifteen clients in each of the three levels; the numbers fluctuated based on incoming clients and their needs.

My mother would be in the first level until the state psychiatrist, who came once every two weeks, could evaluate her further. The van was late and did not arrive until almost 6:00 p.m. I had been waiting since 8:00 a.m. I wanted to be there early to observe the facilities and speak to her new case manager. I tried to be very calm and reassuring for my mother, but all I really wanted to do was throw up. The case manager, with me by her side, presented the form my mother had to sign before the van would depart. My mother refused to sign. I begged the case manager to please give me some time alone with my mother, which she did. My mother was still paranoid and concerned that everything that I was involved in on her behalf was illegal, and I would be arrested. However, because my mother trusted me, even through her mental fog of delusions, I was able to convince her to sign. The thing that convinced my mother to sign was the fact that I could visit her whenever I wanted. My mother arrived with the antipsychotic and antidepressant drugs that the doctors at Florida State Hospital had prescribed. When the visiting psychiatrist made his regularly scheduled visit, he would evaluate her and adjust her medications accordingly.

In my eight hours at the facility prior to my mother's arrival, I had had the opportunity to observe all the clients in levels I and II and what their typical day was like. None of the clients was violent or acted out, at least while I was there. They were, of course, each on the antipsychotic, antidepressant drugs prescribed for them by the visiting psychiatrist. Level I clients had a room and a partial bathroom (basin and toilet) that they shared with a roommate of their own sex and showers that they shared with all patients. Level II clients also shared rooms, but due to the restrictions of the building, all level II clients had to share one bathroom with multiple showers, toilets, and basins. The facility was clean, but it was very old. The furnishings were mostly donated, and some were quite worn. It was nicer than Florida State Hospital, though. Given my mother's circumstances, it was the only game in town.

Between 1986 and 2006, my mother would be housed at all levels of this facility, be taken to a psychiatric hospital when she decompensated, and be evaluated by and returned to the facility, possibly at a lower level. Once, they released her entirely. Before her release I assisted her in purchasing a mobile home where she would live for years before suffering another psychotic break. However, even though she had previously been at the mental facility nearby, when she suffered another psychotic break, she could not just return there. She would have to be admitted to the psychiatric hospital. The Baker Act would have to be ordered by a judge visiting the hospital, using the information obtained from the hospital psychiatrists, and then she would be evaluated for seventy-two hours and returned to another level. This continued until about 2000, when I was forced to sell my mother's mobile home so that all my mother's monthly social security income, except for fifty dollars of personal money, could be given to the facility for her care and housing. This was based on her ability to pay. The facility had allowed my mother to keep her mobile home and pay the necessary utilities and lot rent for many years until it was evident she might not be able to return there. At that point, my mother had been in level III, which afforded her the most independence, for many years without any visits to what they all called the "psych hospital"—a very good thing, I thought. When I visited back then, she used to say quite often, "I wish I would die. I hate living here; there's nothing else left for me." I'd return to Orlando where I would be depressed until I could visit her again.

Eight

In 2005, my mother had been complaining that her lower back hurt and had been to see the physician's assistant, who had prescribed naproxen, a nonsteroidal anti-inflammatory medication, for her on a daily basis. This helped at first, but soon, she began complaining to me that her back was hurting again, even after having been on naproxen for about a year. She went back to the physician's assistant, who could find no problems with her back X-rays, but she continued taking naproxen. I, of course, never having taken naproxen, assumed it was fine to take, even on a long-term basis. In March 2006, it also appeared to me that my mother was mentally decomposing again, and I spoke at length to the head of level III about the possibility of her return to the local psychiatric hospital. However, because my mother lay down in the hall of the level III facility and stated she could not get up because of her back, the head of the facility called 911 to have her taken to the local nonpsychiatric hospital. There, the admitting physician in the ER ordered blood work and so on and had her transferred to a room because of a diagnosis of sepsis. I went into the room, and my mother was prone on the bed. Not only was she not walking, but she was also not talking to anyone, including me. The nurse gave me the quick sepsis diagnosis. I asked to speak to the admitting physician, but he had gone for the day. I immediately told the nurses and anyone who would listen to me that my mother was mentally ill, and because she couldn't walk, she could be physically ill as well. I told them she had been complaining of back ache for some time, and she'd been on naproxen for a very long time. I requested they have their staff psychiatrist visit her. I was told their staff psychiatrist was in Europe, and no one else was available. My mother's psychiatrist from the facility she was in did not have staff privileges at this nonpsychiatric hospital. That evening, I called the ER physician's service and requested that he call me at home, which he did. I once again explained that my mother might be having another psychotic break in addition to having something physically wrong with her. He insisted that my mother was simply refusing to walk or talk, and therefore, once the sepsis infection was cleared up, she would be released...to me. I explained that her residence since 1986 had been the local mental facility. The physician did not want to talk to me and recommended I talk to the hospital's social worker instead.

The next day, I went to the hospital where I did talk to a social worker who had been assigned to my mother's case. She told me, "You will have to carry your mother out of here today [March 9, 2006] because Medicare won't pay for a nursing home." I questioned why she could not simply go back to the mental facility she'd been living at since 1986 and was informed that she could not go back there because she was required to be able to walk or to get in and out of a wheelchair by herself in order to go back there or to the psych hospital. She then insisted that my mother was simply being difficult, and that she could walk and talk but was refusing to do so. Therefore, there was nothing they could do for her. I persisted, asking if they had conclusively determined that there was nothing physically wrong with her, except for the sepsis infection. The social worker once again said that they had and that the sepsis had cleared up. I repeated that something was wrong and insisted that she be seen by a psychiatrist. However, everything I said was seemingly ignored.

I decided to contact the hospital administrator about this situation, which seemed ridiculous to me. I was told that the administrator was out of the country, but I could see the risk management representative. I poured my heart out to this person whose whole job was avoiding the risk of lawsuits. I insisted on having a psychiatrist called in, even if the staff psychiatrist wasn't available. She finally agreed to that, and the hospital found a psychiatrist to evaluate my mother. After this occurred, the risk manager told me my mother was still going to be released to me. Once again, I was thrown back into desperation, trying to comprehend what they were saying to me. Surely, the psychiatrist called in would report that my mother needed to be Baker Acted again and returned to the psychiatric hospital in town. As it turned out, because my mother refused to talk to the psychiatrist, the report simply reflected that my mother was being uncooperative, and there was nothing they could do but release her from the hospital to me. I then demanded all my mother's medical records since her admittance there and threatened a malpractice suit against the hospital. The risk assessment staff member was now listening to me. I was assigned a new social worker who attempted to find a facility that could house my mother.

I was repeatedly told there was nothing wrong with my mother, which I knew to be incorrect. I just didn't know what was wrong with her, and the hospital was obviously washing its hands of the whole situation. I insisted that the admitting ER physician had not done every test necessary to determine why her back might be hurting and causing her to refuse to walk. My concerns continued to be disregarded while the social worker attempted to find a nursing home that would accept her, now that she was immobile. Even though the hospital refused to acknowledge that she was in psychosis *and* possibly physically ill, no nursing homes could be located that could accept her because of her previous mental illness—catch-22. So there were no psychiatric nursing homes in Florida?

I found it disturbing, especially because I was told over and over that the psychiatric hospital where she had been many times could not admit her due to her refusal to walk. I returned to Orlando, only to be phoned at 3:00 a.m. the next day and informed that my mother was vomiting blood and had bloody diarrhea, and they needed my permission to do an endoscopy.

Nine

When I arrived at the hospital, the gastroenterologist informed me that my mother had a bleeding duodenal ulcer and would need surgery to correct it. However, her vital signs were not strong enough for surgery, so they'd have to wait and see when they could operate. She was now in intensive care and on a ventilator because of the endoscopy. She was awake and alert but with many tubes inserted to catch the blood continuing to flow from the bleeding ulcer. I immediately focused on the severity of the ulcer and asked the physician what to expect. He was frank with me and told me that for her to be operated on, her vital signs needed to improve, and the possibility did exist that she might die because the ulcer had just been discovered, even though she had been in the hospital for almost two weeks and nothing had been found to be wrong with her.

I immediately called my brother in Pensacola and told him that he needed to come because she might die. He arrived the next day. We sat with her and waited for the physicians to appear on their rounds for two days. My brother stayed in a local motel, and I drove back to Orlando. Before I left the next morning, the hospital called me and told me that my mother's condition had worsened. I called my brother at the motel and told him to go to the hospital immediately and I'd arrive within the hour. I can only thank God that my mother lived long enough for us both to be by her side when she passed away. More importantly, she knew we were there. As her vital signs continued to worsen, the nurses were planning to resuscitate her if her heart failed. I had given the hospital a copy of my mother's living will as soon as she was admitted, and I informed the intensive care nurse of this. The nurse insisted that no such directive was in her medical records, and my mother would be resuscitated. This was in addition to all the heartbreak my family had already endured through this whole horrible experience. All I could think about was what I kept hearing my mother say to me when we were at the lake, watching stupid people feed the alligators. She'd said, "It's not the alligators' fault. They don't know they're monsters." It occurred to me that my mother had always thought her mental illness made her a monster, because so many people had treated her like one without really understanding the affliction properly.

When her heart gave out in intensive care, I crawled across her on the bed crying, "I love you, Mama!" in between screams that this was not the way it was supposed to end: so horribly; blood coming out of her mouth; so much fighting with the hospital, physician, and social workers; so many angry words and threats; so many pleas for the hospital to see that something was physically wrong from the very beginning.

Ten

I spent the next year of my life attempting to have the ER physician, psychiatric physician, and social worker/nurse found culpable in my mother's death but to no avail. I consulted a lawyer first and was told that I could not sue on my mother's behalf unless I depended on her for my income, which I didn't. The next step was to file formal complaints against each of these people with the Florida Department of Health. I filed the complaints in April 2006, only one month after my mother's death. I cannot begin to explain the bureaucracy that ensnared me for the next year. First, the individual complaints had to go to the Division of Medical Quality Assurance Bureau of Consumer and Investigative Services in Tallahassee, Florida. After more than a year of being bounced from one prosecution services unit and office of general counsel to another, I received two letters: one for the psychiatric physician and one for the social worker/nurse. I was so discouraged that I gave up my pursuits against the ER physician and decided against filing additional information on the other two complaints.

The last correspondence I had against the ER physician was dated January 5, 2007, which stated that the investigation of the complaint was still ongoing in the Gainesville office. As I recall, I attempted to contact the Gainesville office to ask about the status of the complaint and was told the same thing that the letter regarding the psychiatric physician had informed me in January 2007: "Please be advised that the complaint you filed in the matter referenced above has been investigated and reviewed by the Probable Cause Panel of the Board of Medicine. Pursuant to Section 456.073(2), Florida statutes, the panel directed the case to be dismissed."

The letter I received for the complaint against the social worker/nurse stated, "The afore-referenced case was presented to the Probable Cause Panel for the Board of Nursing. After reviewing the entire investigative file, including the uniform complaint, witness statements, and the relevant records, the Probable Cause Panel has made the determination to close this case without a finding of probable cause."

I was also informed that "Pursuant to Chapter 456, Florida Statutes, you have sixty (60) days from the receipt of this notification to provide ANY ADDITIONAL information to the Probable Cause Panel, which may be relevant to the Panel's decision. If the information provided is determined to be relevant, the case will be re-presented to the Panel for a reconsideration of whether or not probable cause exists."

Last, regarding the complaint against the psychiatric physician, I was advised, "Because this case was dismissed without a finding of probable cause, the complaint and investigative file is confidential and exempt from the Florida Sunshine Law pursuant to Section 456.073(10), Florida Statutes. Information about the complaint and the investigation will not be disclosed to the public without the subject's written permission."

I had spent a year not only grieving my mother's death but also being reminded of how she had died and how she was treated by the medical community of a major hospital. I had no energy left to fight the bureaucracy any longer. Instead, I devoted my energy to this book and my mother's poetry. My mother was an intelligent, kind, loving person and deserved better. I hope no one who reads this book will ever have to go through this with a loved one. However, I plead with each of you to be a health-care advocate for the mentally ill in your families. Even with an advocate, as my mother had, the system is against you.

As to my own mental health, in 1998 I was diagnosed with depression and obsessive-compulsive disorder. I have been under a psychiatrist's care and taking Prozac ever since.

Eleven

I cannot be certain when my mother wrote the rest of the poetry she left me, but I know for sure that once she was hospitalized for the first time, she wrote no more poetry. The remainder of my mother's poems appears in this chapter.

Unnamed

Once in a dream I traveled through space
To a mystical, magical, faraway place—
And all of the people there were you,
And every wish, wished came true.

And I asked myself, what place is this?
What part of outer space is this?
Then I awoke and there you were
And I looked at you and knew the answer.

Of a Duchess Growing Old

Still the essence of great romance
Clings about her like the smoke
With which the burning autumn leaves
Their bare-branched trees encloak.

Exit Before Midnight

In four years longer,
And then four more,
She would have been forty—
And then forty-four.

And the thought of growing older
Must have seemed too sad
To one who felt that her beauty
Was all she ever had.

(My mother told me that "Exit before Midnight" was written when Marilyn Monroe committed suicide.)

Grand Finale

The panorama of sunset
When day is done
Is the Grand finale
Second to none

www.ingramcontent.com/pod-product-compliance
Lightning Source LLC
Chambersburg PA
CBHW070556290526
45790CB00002B/713